THE ALCHEMY OF BLOOD

THE ALCHEMY OF BLOOD

Poems

Richard LaBrie

Wealtown Press

Wealtown Press, 65 N. Madison Ave., Suite 707, Pasadena, CA 91101
wealtownpress.com

Published 2026 by Wealtown Press

Credits: Cover art and photo, author photo, and book design by Richard LaBrie. Excerpts by Stéphane Mallarmé and Anton Wildgans are in the public domain; translated by Jean-Marie Martz and used by permission. Excerpt by Voltaire and the translation by William F. Fleming are in the public domain. Excerpt by Fernando Pessoa is in the public domain; translated by Marcel Camargo and used by permission. William Stafford, excerpt from "AnyTime" from *The Way It Is: New and Selected Poems*. Copyright ©1970, 1998 by William Stafford and the Estate of William Stafford. Reprinted with the permission of The Permissions Company, LLC on behalf of Graywolf Press, Minneapolis, Minnesota, graywolfpress.org.

10 9 8 7 6 5 4 3 2 1
First Edition

Identifiers:
ISBN 979-8-9934746-0-1 (print, alk. paper)
ISBN 979-8-9934746-1-8 (ebook)
LCCN: 2025922429 (print)

Wealtown Press is committed to the principle that creative output evolves from mind, body, spirit, psychological, and collective and individual consciousness pathways. Protecting the freedom of this universal modality is crucial.

This book is printed in China by Union Printing Company, LTD, on acid-free paper.

For my mother and father,
and for those who still bother to pay attention

Contents

Citrinitas

Rubedo

Preface

Scary and hot, alchemy is fun. Rooted in early science, then pseudo-science, then philosophy and psychology. I'm grateful it is a thing, because in looking at and arranging this collection, I was surprised at the disparate nature of the work. Alchemy allowed me to find a structure, thanks to Carl Jung's separation of the concept of change and growth into the four stages of fiery transformation: Nigredo (blackening, ash, death), Albedo (whitening, rebirth, early insight), Citrinitas (yellowing, dawning of wisdom), and Rubedo (reddening, wholeness, enlightenment). The book is in the order of the four stages, so it begins with the deathlike tone of the Nigredo section. Each section, like every stage of life's changes, has its challenges and scorches and darknesses. I hope you can stay with the collection through the fourth section, which I'm hoping brings relief. And I'm hoping you see some humor even in some of the raw embers here.

Disparateness is not to be disparaged; it's all around us. My work with people in psychotherapy has taught me that. Every person interfaces with the world and with me in a unique way. And just as I cannot control what comes to me in that work—nor would I want to—I cannot control the dream state that begins in the formation of a poem. Perhaps I bristle against, or feel bored by, a singular approach to anything. Life is too full for that.

Why would a psychologist write poetry? Psychotherapy requires me to form a third eye: on me, on the client, on the world. But it's not omniscient. Only looking. It turns, peers. Fifteen years ago I needed to begin evoking or expelling or digesting what I came across in the world and in consult with other souls. These poems started appearing. That is the context. No specific client info is shared.

Engaging in psychotherapy vibrates hard—as does just surviving this first quarter century (or any?). So, the vibrations leak out. I also feel compelled to say that the "I" in a poem is not always me, or sometimes it is, but who cares? The facts here are not facts. Do what you wish with them. Let them hit you. Stéphane Mallarmé's words inspire my trance and permit its output:

"Paint, not the thing, but the effect it produces."

What is here is what dropped in, especially impacted by our collective experiences this past 10 years. Be brave. Make your own brew of it. Re-fire it for yourself. Your interpretation is the most valuable one.

Richard LaBrie
2026

Note 1: A few of the poems in this collection deal with intense or triggering content. If you or someone you know is struggling, help is available. You can connect with compassionate and trained individuals by calling or texting 988 anytime in the US and Canada. In the UK, you can call 111. If you are in a different area from these, please check your local resources.

Note 2: Although I work as a psychologist, these pages are offered as poetry, not as psychotherapy or clinical guidance.

THE ALCHEMY OF BLOOD

Nigredo

What is deemed to shine must first bear to burn.
—Anton Wildgans

Sweet Child of Mine

My dead father wrote me a letter through the ether, oddly
suffused with detailed imagery of old white men's ear hair.
Crusty tan-green wax-twirls into darkness.
He wrote that these were the ears of men of industry
who'd been told repeatedly
of the universal dangers of their products.
He confirmed that the men's dismissals
of this information
were truly narcissistic defenses.

His voice in writing became louder:
They are responsible. Take action. It's OK to kill them.

He said nowadays some will be young and of color,
with trimmed ears. Or women.
No matter.
Hang them all on a zip line
over the Grand Canyon and ask them politely
to change their ways.
When they don't, let them drop. It's the only way.

My father was a kind man –
a moderately conservative mild capitalist.

How surprising as I sit at my sunless breakfast!

A Veil of Spring

The oil barge adrift on the horizon,
black against the vacationers'
yellow beach light.

I laughed, and wondered
if it's our mercy ship,
even as helicopters raced overhead.

Their rumble matched the tenuousness
rippled beneath our skin,
and the reality beyond my pale joke.

Happy Valentine's Day, 1985

I am the kind of depressed that makes a
  woman want to fuck another man

This, the thought, as I stay in my bunker
The chalk of the cement parching my
  fingertips

I touch my index to my tongue
Seeking its pH
To confirm my dry imbalance

Perhaps flesh is not the container
  to trap these bones

Deconstruction

Money Man was angry.
Pushing, yelling, pushing.
Jimmy put a screwdriver through
   Money Man's temple.
It was hot.
He was hungry.
We all were.

Oh, Jimmy, channel of the heat.
Tell us of the underside of release.
Make us your servants for serving us.
You opened the vault.

8%! 8%!! 8%!!!
Money Man screamed as if we could
   follow his rants about the leveraged financing.
Lost he was, under the boot leather
   of Adam Smith's prefrontal cortex's
   stomps on his throat's howling pulse of
   need need need.

Jimmy scrambled Money Man's cortex,
   like eggs, into a state no longer
   suitable for the Keynesian subsidies
   of the egg supply stream of America.

I mean, the lumber subsidies?

.

.

.

.

It doesn't matter.
13 other buildings will go up around
   this crime scene.
Jimmy will die in prison.
We will work again after the
   investigation.

In a year I will be hammering next door.
My $6 food truck breakfast burrito
   will cost $8 by then.
I will leverage to meet that 33% increase
   for the egg and potato sack
   from my 2% salary increase.

The developers will have made
   their 33% profit.
I will sit on the gypsum-powdered grass patch
   and eat, and weep.
Or not.

The Whittler

So many for him to disappoint
Cave inward
And carve affect into wood
Nick and flick brings order
Hold tight

The wood
Does not disappoint
Its fibers ignorant of his plight
Generous to his supplication
It forgives

His feint
That he does not care
To disappoint the lives
Of those many other hearts
He does

He cares
Yet winces from the burn
And fades into the dusk
To disappoint himself away
   from the vibrancy
Of risk

Qualitative Data Collected at Parnassus

– Setting:
Every Stanza ever written in the world is
gathered in a convention hall. Their Poet Masters
are sequestered silently outside.

– Question 1 (baseline):
Why do your Poet Masters use you to stave off suicide?
Stanzas ignored the question – immediately began
arguing about form, spacing, rhythm, rhyme,
and justifying margin justification.
No Stanza seemed to hear the gunshots over the shouting,
culling the population of Masters they were there to save.
Associated Stanzas vanished in sync.
Estimated losses: 20%.

– Question 2 (adjusted for scenario):
Is a blank space of lines considered a Stanza?
More shouting as more blank spaces appeared
directly following distant gunshots.
One Stanza wondered whether changing ink color
was acceptable, and was instantly punched
flat in the period, then vanished after a gunshot.
Some Stanzas teamed up.
Some mentioned previous hurts at previous conventions.
The Villanelles stood smugly off to the side.
Translations stared at Originals, some
with apparent admiration, some inquisitively,
some with hostility.
Debates on form appeared to outweigh devotion
to their Masters, who continued to die – the gunshots
instant precursors to Stanza blanknesses.
Estimated losses: 80%

– Question 3 (shouted over rapid gunfire):
Is the subjective objective or is the objective subjective?
A Septuagenarian Stanza on typewriter paper shouted
that decades ago a 1960s-era Pink Panther cartoon
showed the animal vacuuming the dirty ground and then,
seeing his own tail as a targetable piece of doggerel,
turned the vacuum toward his tail and began sucking
himself up into it. The vacuum continued up his body,
arm, and into itself, until both vanished with a pop.
The Septuagenarian then caught fire. Convention hall cleared.
– End of data collected.
– Interpretive results likely in 6 months.
– Primary investigators report no conflicts of interest.

Disco

I wore cotton in the 70s and 80s
Something seemed wrong about all the polyester
Cotton – natural, durable
I had heard when plastic burns it creates a poison,
  something like cyanide
Hitler's breath

Now I wear joggers
Poly and whatever
Because I don't give a fuck
I am as bad as the MBA investment bankers of the 80s
  in their track suits

No, they didn't not care the same way I don't care
I don't care in a worse way

Because they won by making me not care
They won because my hatred won
And now they're old and retired and drunk and rich
And I am soon nowhere to be found

Because I will light the pants on fire
And inhale the retched history of your greed
Rock the boat, baby

Apology

I saw a certain kind of darkness, and it made me expect more of the world.
That is a bad expectation, destined for disappointment.
So I walked into those woods, a tree stead hiding moist lumber and plaster and nails.
Broken, old, a stench of rust and the blood from knees pressed to the crumbled hearth.

I made a pact and for ten years stayed in the pavilion of 3am and its tremors.
I no longer exited, and forbid safety to seduce me, for it had only made me more scared.
A decade of drift, to whatever place my body said no to.
No natural evil to bring, so I carried vengeance, righteousness, even as I pummeled.

Deep male voices of unencumbered, impulsive, reckless force drew me to them.
The old split second of hesitance to engage my rage had vanished.
For a decade the pure joy of pulverizing their stupidity with my body was unchecked.
I was them, and not, because knowing the knowing of my actions, I was unlike them.

The knees on the hearth of that smashed house sought warmth or penitence or answers.
The blood I later spilled and bled was not the same, but was my foreclosure on life's mist.
The mist that is possible, for some, after a transmutative cataclysm, is a fresh morning.
My ten years left only a kind of tinnitus of fog too heavy and sharp and harsh to inhale.

Revenants like me walk among you, gray in aura, grim in jaw, eyes quick to assess and flee.
Don't reach for us through your goodism unless you are prepared to sponge up the mess.
But, if you do, kneel first, in a better way than I had, for you will need holy protection.
Or, leave us be.

Accretion

If I were a caterpillar in that flimsy box,
grabbed by those bus-stop boys and flung to the ground,
I would have sped up time to molt and spin and fly away.

If I were me, in the moment, and not dissociated away,
I would have grown bigger and protected the box
or beat those boys senseless.

If I were me, now, I would be forced to mitigate the conflict
and find resolution, given my place in society.

But I was none of that.

My uncle could be himself,
and the next day come with his stature and his 300 pounds
and his dense beard. He scared those tow-headed
buzz-top boys senseless.

The second box of caterpillars lived. But still,
there is an unresolved chord in this song…

> My PF Flyers, washed and perfectly laced,
> prepped for show-and-tell,
> gleaming with my simple pride,
> could not alone protect that first box –
>
> the fuzzy soft unborn wing-set of potential.

The Fragility of the Dahlia Stem in the Psychotherapist's Office

I will not curate this
What they told me, my charge
I'll not protect the legacy of our organism, my species

Somewhere right now a man slides
his finger tongue or penis into a baby or child
or young girl or boy

Or a woman does it

Over and over

And over
time the entrained fawning coquettishness
that belies the fractured young self
begins performing for the monster

I know this because they told me
all of them in this sacred space
in parallel process and detailed
patterns so vividly clear as to smudge doubt into shit
To smear that brown truth into their abuser's souls

They escaped and I was supposed to help them mend

But oh, how I wanted to kill the monsters
Then my quiet rage mangled the empathic balance
Scaring my quaking charge at times
Or energizing them with the berry of my validation

Validation did not matter – I was already gone
Drifted into my own viciousness
Setting a course to fail them
The salted slime blood of revenge an ethical misfire

They come to me shaking
Then realize they are alone
The slap-back echo of their voice a parching breeze
I'm off, fighting the war they exited

Abandoned again, their courage snuffs my cowardice
like the thumb they now must use to kill the candle
of the hope I stole –
the char of my seething useless vigilantism

Wabi Sabi

You will get extra days
Using your smart iron and glass
Our plastics are in me
Festering and waiting
To take me
Maybe like my mother
Surprised, then dead in 6 days

We used up everything
Like the wise Buddhist said
But it was unwise
Leeching over and over into us
While our good intentions told us—
Good!

Don't save me when the time comes
I'm properly used up
So, I'm good, yes
Eco-friendly
In my state of cellular pollution
That eats me to nothing
Like a worn-down rag

Success

Tug

(For E.)

I was born a suicide
Well, no
I once had arms-up pride
Glazy wonder
Flappy little hands over skin and food and toys

Then, no
Outside the circle
Push
Grab
Taunt
Hit
Kick
Blab
Steal
Shame
Break
Leave
Swell
Twat
Dick
Cunt
Prick
Ridicule

.

.

.

.

.

.

.

.

.

Then, you
All
How
Us
This species
Our gifts
How could you
All
Not all
Some
Don't care
All
Run
Nowhere
Outside in
Want
Can't
Want
More

.

.

.

.

.

.

.

.

.

.

Then, there is this:
What dragged weight is too heavy?
All the years pulled, pushed, hidden, polished
We don't tell ourselves to breathe
No need
We tell ourselves to stay
Need
To
Every
Fucking
Day

What dragged weight is too heavy?
What dragged weight is too heavy?

Endemic

(February, 2022)

I envy the dead
Sauntering around me, fretless
With not enough cells to carry rage
Or misanthropy
Like I do

I am tired.
23 months and many decades
To shed enough of my cells just short of
Oblivion
But perfect for enlightenment, like the
Monks
… indeed, I have failed

It won't be so bad
Take the rest (of the cells)
Let me flit unbothered around some other's anger
Keep your brick-like convictions
Shove them

Carbon Options

They say the planetary roller screws are coming in jumbo lots.
I am so excited!
They move in all directions so smoothly.
Just like my elbows and wrists!
They'll be housed in the robots that will make our life
  so much more efficient.
We'll work less. Just like the computers made us work less.
And the internet.

I am so excited! They'll be expensive, but I will pay.
What confounding reason do any of us even have to bother
  ejaculating into a mate anymore?
Everything is going to be fine.
I do hope I'm invited to watch a TED talk.
I want to see the bearded man in the skinny jeans with no tie
  tell me how to be.
I am forever embracing. I believe in you all!
Take me. Take me home. Make me whole.

There'll be no more anti-fancy fight against this when they see
  the stainless steel and titanium will be so, so silky.
I can't even eat, because it's time to look for
  the stock IPO that I need to buy for the robots.
For the gleaming nano metal future.
For all that will breathe for us.
Stop fighting, all of you!
I am so excited!
Thanks be.

Albedo

It is not more suprising to be born twice than once; everything in nature is resurrection.

—Voltaire

Now, Dust

A solid thick cover over my truth
And my connection to beauty
Buried long ago
With the pulsing joy my smiling face displayed

To the world I am smooth
But sidelong in my glances
Open me
My inners jagged, obscure

Suspension

Looking up, I knew the clouds could not keep me aloft.

But if I fell from a plane, the beauty of the mist
  should be able to hold me,
  to counter millennia of magnetic reality.

Why not?
Why not burn my fealty to groundedness
  with gradated pillows of contrast and glow?
Why not hope?

A psychologist once told me that hope
  is the mechanism of the helpless child.

Crusty eyelashes, I awaken young in a seat – car or plane?
The searing afternoon ochre blinks me.

Are we there yet?

The Liminal

I don't trust things
that don't rot
like robots and plastic wood.

Ask my great, great, great, great, great, great
grandchildren.
They'll respond if they can
through the trachs in their throats
because they ate the vegetables
they tried to grow in their soil.

I imagine them saying in surprise,
What the fuck?
Why the tumor from the carrot?
But of course, that's what I'm saying now.
They won't grow them then
because they'll already know,
because they'll be smart,
because, hey, science.

Is this too dark?
Ok, well, I love
my great, great, great, great, great, great grandchildren
already.
I just wish I could help them
to even know
from here and now…

of the real and squishy
of the weak after the strong
of the continual bending
of every cell
to the inevitable end
that makes it all, us all,
in constant straddle
between the now
and our vaporous
organic truth.

Self-Assessment to the HR Manager

I wanna be on LaBrea and feel like shit
Blow a guy in a car
Use my dumpster fried chicken grease
    mouth to exhaust the day month year
Walk the sunburn sidewalk till I fall
Curl up on cardboard
Clutch my jeans behind my thighs
    cotton stiff with my issue
My final pith incalculable
            on your spreadsheet

Evel Knievel

He'd come to the suburbs
For a post-event promo rally
After some jump I couldn't attend
I was 11

Humid heat wicked the sweat down off
  my elbow from my armpits
My polyester tee too tight
My puberty smell shameful and new
Every experience tunneled in embarrassment

But I liked motorcycles
I rode, too – a Honda XR-75
Alone in the woods, a crazy little thing capable of 60 mph
To survive the 70s is like a candy fever dream
  you didn't deserve

I had been rehearsing how to ask my mother
  to buy me my first deodorant
A growing child still, but I could nail the clutch
  and 4-speed gearbox
    around a field of shorn wheat,
      sliding perfectly through turns
Life and risk and dreams of muscles
  as I hid from my body odor

Evel said stuff, people cheered, he was above me
  on the makeshift carnival stage and I liked the leather
  but the cape was questionable

Leaving childhood in the recognition of my armpit reek
  froze me for long moments
Newly considering my corporeal presence on Earth
Caught in a toggle between my looming adult power and death,
  because I could see the leap now–
Child—adult—dead.

Standing below the leathered man who defied it over buses
A yell broke my tunnel vision
Someone said heart attack
Time crunched and they carried a middle-aged man past me
  toward fairground medics
His face purple, still, bouncing against the jolts of their carry

I don't know what Evel said
His cape useless to the stilled man
His legend a benefit to us
Flying, flying with intention
  into the hope of a better landing

Regular Vows

Cheesecake on W. 4th St. you had to order me to go be normal and have a meal to get out of the apartment to get out of my head. You tried to train me to tolerate myself.

When I come back next time I will be more normal or as my friend's seven-year-old says, "regular." I will eat and not ponder things beyond my reach. I will drive the 5 to a gated community. I will accept the uniform colors of the lap siding in the development. I will stream the bell curve of the music of my cohort. I will sleep OK and eat the salted meat and grab for what is there. I will watch Oprah and cooking shows and joke about wine o'clock and be OK with most things. I will be regular. I will not hate myself for not being regular and I will not hate the regulars. I will be satisfied with the median and the mean. Can the ego die before the body? I don't think so. That's why I have to wait until I come back because on the other side I will kill the ego and then *then!* I will come back and I will be id and I will be regular and I will take what I want and I will not worry and I will not think beyond the concrete and I will shake my hips.

There is much work to be done.

Phone Call

You hold the happy together
I want to break it
Unveil your blindness
Yet
To speak to you I weep
At your probable wisdom
Because who said my sombre is wise?

The squirrel I accidentally killed
Has sad friends now
But others jump for the peanuts
Play in the trees

I don't get it
I should have
That's what they always said

Hey, how did you know?

Not Quite Bipolar

My eyes are too big for my stomach
and I see things inside that I then want
to manifest and I want too much of all
of that and my ideas are flighting around
and I'm wanting to turn them into
colorful solids and my pressure is often
mounting but I sleep OK and I'm only
sometimes irritable and human hands
are amazing and so is the whole body
and nature too and how can one just sit
and slump and tune out when there is all
this emerald shiny beauty – but maybe
I have the sickness and maybe I don't – or
maybe this is simply an expansiveness
that's necessary to just get through it all…
no… necessary to dream it, see it,
walk it, grab it, be it, them, you, me, us.

Formerly of the Ages

used to
be
not scared

puma paws
confident
deep indent
the dirt

scale a
boulder
garden

for a
breathed
mauve
view

used to be

Seeking

All the ones
Crawling, walking
Beating hearts through whatever skin

Eyes in search
Connecting, rejecting
Scaling fears and walking in

To arms of sun
Melting, curling
Feeling home and ending the Lenten

Of dark air
Drying, searing
Disorganized from the rhythm of warm din

In silent question
Staring, tearing
Aware of the scold and sully of skin

Turning it off
Yes, no
Holding still for the soft footsteps, in

Taking us out
Freeing, confusing
Knowing there are too many to love

Flaw

My tree branch leaf veins'
Sweet and spoiled brine passed to you
Pray the pain is tamped

If Only I Burn

I am screaming-not-screaming at the alchemist
accusing it of fakery

--I want the turmeric sunlight rather
than the flat black of mid-sleep

-----You can't escape the white burn
of rebirth

--Fuck you

The forge shuts down
cooling quicker than reality

* * *

Awake…
The stream the podcast the magazine the book
make me believe change comes
by cooing a succulent
cupping an Eastern tea
self-accounting by a cool stream
a pistachio paste recipe
and
reading your Substack
transferring my entirety into your imago
Here, take my routing number

* * *

Nope, still not awake…
Indignation and rage
in a dream jail
ash and leaden chest

--Then fire that thing up and smoke me out to nothing

-----Attaboy!… No

Heat like a heart attack
this fucker won't kill me
won't let me skip ahead out of
this forge of eternity

* * *

Abduct me scrape me away
your theory is a lie
my ash can't pop white
Your charcoal burn to magnesium flare
is the luring of the parent-god
its selfish pride in me
its threat

--Don't you know I have already been alive?
Just give me what's next but I'll not go down
the birth canal again. Skip me to golden futures
or end me.

----- … *[silence]*

* * *

It's gone I am alone
beyond forge to plasma
a selfish dream
because
where are the people?

The highest temperature is called Planck
Big Bang beyond plasma
will I feel pain or do I fear pain or fear fear of pain?

* * *

Ribbons of brown like audio recording tape
float in a star stream and scare the shit
out of me
I sleep-walk to the neighbors' house
psychic in finding my parents
I'm 5 or 8
or dead then alive
or just in need of my people

Thank you, Bob Mould

The night-blooming jasmine still smelled like possibility
to me in Los Angeles in 1989. An open canvas.
A separation from my rough edges in Philadelphia.
A year before climate warnings. Summer evenings
were still cool, and so different from the East Coast.
I could be reborn. May 19, I perched at McCabe's
and watched you finish "See a Little Light"
in blazing a cappella, and then apologize to us.
I saw you break down after "Hardly Getting Over It,"
turn, grab the handrail as you ran upstairs away from
the audience. The angle of your hand on the rail creased
our worship, increased it, your sweet toddler self showing,
bent at the waist, a stomach-ache fold, your Strat
momentarily a precious toy, the outer flesh of your
left palm squeezed against that rail as you stooped
up the stairs. We were not confused. 120 patient civilians
paused easily in the collective and then you returned with
"Brasilia Crossed With Trenton." This was pure open
vulnerability, 36 years before today's char
of fear crossed with bombast.
I think you are the bravest person I ever saw.

Citrinitas

My soul is an unseen orchestra;
I don't know what instruments,
what range or size comprise it –
violins and harps, cymbals and drums –
I don't know what lies inside me.
I only hear the symphony.
—Fernando Pessoa

Self Help

(For C.)

We are getting to the age of forgetting
Forgetting we are forgetting, so
It's easier
A sadness now fleeting
   into a slip
      that's not sad

A drift
The kind of relaxed,
   the kind of lazy,
      I had wished for in the middle years

The carelessness of the less self-aware
Now a gift
Absolved of fussiness
No fussing with
   that outed string of twinkle lights,
      that habit that isn't quite one now,
         that goal

What goal?
Is this living in the present?
Is it mindfulness?

I turn to you
Stunned that I can just be here
Without lament

Apollo Sends Regrets to the Masses

(After "Team" *by Lorde)*

I am not very Dionysian. I have tried.
Tried to fit in with all those funsters and
their genitals and their alcohol whoops
of joy. My sinking into contemplation
does not seem to elicit raised-arm dancing.
You walked away, like so many others,
with that angle to your hanging head
that indicates escape. The kind from which
you don't look back. And yet, I was not
depressed in my stoic ponderments.
Or in any of my breathed moments
with any of you. But I can apparently
really sling that swarthy feeling at y'all –
the unintended sticky slothy outcome
of my seriousness – like pasty cold oatmeal
hitting you. I guess I apologize?

Perhaps my body will throb one day like yours
and people will think I'm happy even though
I already am. But then they will be happy too.
So there.

Ectopic Rupture in the Neosphere

The Mockingbird sounds like a car alarm
  an innocent, accepting kind of grace

The 30,000 parts of a car screech
  a blueprint for its secure mating whoop

Females flit to him with rational heat
  his pure environmental mastery

A lizard darts by

An AI named Chuck spouts to the last few
  but we don't sing to his stolen man-voice

Chuck's boudoir throat belies metallic blood
  we are not in his dry trees anymore

Man, 22, Plays House

She did not invite me into her process as her process was silent
In the end she made a decision with her vagina
Oh me, such a cis-hetero!
My judgment is with my dick
I guess?

I was – am – mean
People will hate this poem

> *Why didn't you guys talk about it?*
> *Well, she never talked and I talked too much,*
> *probably out of anxiety at her silence.*

I called from a distance after leaving the house for a breath
Weeks later, she in a rented room
to quantify her affair
Me on another coast in a sleeping bag on a floor,
to qualify my future

> Me: *I'm moving out.*
> *Please don't, can you come back?*
> *Hmm, are you going to stop seeing him?*
> *No.*

There it was, reality, the conservation of personal resources
above all else – adulthood

When I tell this story now, I break into big laughter – the fun kind
Not crazy pain laughter

More that kind when the belly churns its mirth up
and past any pretense that we make sense

Oh, you grownups! You will get what you want no matter what!
Oh, my naivete! That's the mirth!
Me, you, he, living together?
Or in proximity of your ponderance?
Were you inventing polyamory in the 80s?
It already had been
And I missed it?

I'm not sure I amored anyone
At 22

—

In an epilogue of memory, before the final drift
Beyond my generalized bitterness at human needs
I asked you what you fantasized about his character

What do you imagine he will be like?

You were generous, brave, and shared it with me
An openness about how you also might be naïve in all this

A vision of him, a writer, sitting ascetic with a cat

My sudden calm and your honesty…
we were pups in that moment, caring of our slimness
Knowing there was a field worthy of questioning ahead
questing into it aware of our innocence
aware of the necessary unbridling to come

Traipsing the Littoral

I'll not pet the shark with hands,
but with a stroke of admiration
for its relentless motion,
for its uncuteness

Some guru will tell it to slow,
be still, be mindful

The teeth will come in handy then

Chomp-chomp, you helper
There is only running smooth and cool

Teeth and blood
Because that's how it will go

Intergenerational

Waking slowly one Sunday morning I muttered,

I've inherited your mother's unsaid sorries.

Hmm?

I inhaled and exhaled as if just stirring,
as if I'd spoken in my sleep.

I had not.

But in that moment I understood the torture
of managing the healing of something in our other –
something we did not originally tear,

of being the stand-in of an endless rehearsal
of a play we both hope can find a rewrite
before the curtain,

of the knowledge that this is how we are made –
to couple in this veiled mommy daddy substitution
in our plea for that still-needed soft warm blanket
of the right cloth that does not cut us
like the original blanket that tried not to
but did,
despite its attempts to remove
its own hidden razor shavings
tangled in the weave.

The Epistemology of the Anthropocene, Bruh

Before the fall, great white men in the throes
  of their euphoric ultimateness used their
penises
  freely with the young girls
A sniff and the jolt of coke
Or stock option victories
A skin wrap wriggle zing of life's best minutes ahead
Just before skin hair eyes moistness and fake procreation

She's 14

Ah but now they're gone, those pols
Who is left?
Tech bros
  in burrowed silos
And maybe a woman?

Smart enough – or neurodivergent enough –
  to keep their dicks out of kids
And to pump food and air into
  a polished bunker ahead of the end times
LED sheen in every chamber
A one-way elevator

My advice?
Stop calling yourselves bros
Alone, you can't fuck a baby
  out of your own bleached ass when the oxygen fails

Or if that woman is with you and spits one out,
It will eat you

Temporal

The searing field of white
Which is death
Imposes its slipstream

Early, then always.

A flaming danger
A taboo'd curiosity
A future sanctuary
A relief

The searing field of white
Which is death
Imposes its slipstream

A fear, mitigated by our
  childlike hope
A propellant, chasing our
  eternity
A magnet, welcomed,
  formerly unseen
    as our eternal stanch companion

Superannuation of the Carrier

(For Marshmallow Lumba and her flock, 1996)

Retired compass of the pigeon's beak
Withdrawn, inside
Beyond the moulting's reach
To ossify under scorn

Sequestered memories of soaring
Purposed, loved
Tendered with a vocation not asked for
Accepted, prided

Precise sky arcs once shimmered and
  joyful flaps primed a city, mother,
  doctor, soldier to twist upward,
  expectantly, toward the gentle expert.

Then a voice carried on a wire.

Sudden extended stillness sun to moon
Fazed, freezed
Caged with a pained urge not fathomed
Laid, offed

Fallowed then freed into puzzlement
Directionless, starved
Begrudged the welfare of our crumbs
Labeled, shooed

The beauty of your bloodline overlooked
Dulled, forgotten
Cheated of the dovenly warm glance
Mistaken, exterminated

We remember your skill,
  the original wireless whisper,
  encoded in your lineage,
  silent and wise under your coo.

* * *

Flaked flesh cells swoon on the wind
Lost, aimless
Hard machine metal skin of modernity bears down
Stubborn, confident… permanent

Some lucky few are hobbied.

Color

The specter of the flower haunts us
As it grunts
Expecting us to see its beauty

How does a flower grunt? you say
I say it does
Shut up

I walked with it, the flower
You did, too
And so it goes

What are you talking about? you say
Everything
Anything

Both of us dropped into this field
Seeing the petals
Chewing them differently

Pulled together but not
In the end
Able

February, 1970

He told me the daylight in Maine
   is heavy with its own ending
He did not hide his shaking thumb
Or his fingers thumping the table
In rhythm to some current inside
Maybe a briny churning bodily total
   of his additive anxiety
A life of cold, a fear
Transferred to the wood
Next to the peanuts

Young, I knew everything was salt
Blood, medical saline, our fish sisters
I was not yet nervous
Trying to decode his tapping
   and tempo
To decide when I should begin being so

Clinical Notes, Independent Review

Every nudge and snuggle and ask and grab
is a translation of our languages, asking,
Will I be OK? Will I be alone?

In these days, our pulling together should be
stronger and more frequent as we seek that. Is it?

It is now not enough for my cat to just sit
curled on my lap and be petted. Every few minutes
she stands, climbs my chest, rubs against my face.
Under the adorable is the help cry.

What's going on? What's going on, stinky?
(she does not stink)

I'll assign her two masters degrees, one in public policy,
the other in sociology, with a focus on chaos theory
and social reorganizational patterns. Eventually a PhD
in social psychology. She deserves these honorifics.
Close to my face she will purr to me a warning
that we are in a capitalist system
of Munchausen by Proxy.

Her notes:
Perpetrator diagnosis, ICD-10 code F68.A.
Clinical interview: patient demonstrates
significant lack of insight regarding their
purveyance of products and their requests
for payment, ignorant of the potential for
conditioned responses that create a loop of
financial, emotional, and physical damage
to victim.

Victim diagnosis, ICD-10 code T74.
Patient reports, and observed symptoms demonstrate,
patient born into system requiring labor output
to obtain livable resources in feedback loop
which eventually is unsustainable.
Patient reports becoming victim of social pressures,
cultural expectations, and laws that further deepen
the negative impact of the feedback loop. Patient names
the perpetrator: corporatocracy. Patient expresses
frustration that front desk personnel mocked patient
for using this term during intake.

Clinician leaves exam room, walks to front desk
and smacks staff upside the head.

Upon return, clinician finds the exam room is now an Ark.
A bear captain pilots in co-navigational grace with a condor.
A full ship. The patient lines every surface of the Ark
with a padding of many soft leaves. Clinician sits near water.
A narwhal, an octopus, a dolphin. Clinician weeps.
A cure, not contained in a diagnostic manual. Nonfungible.
The commonweal of a children's book.

The Gemini Capsule

Not quite snakes in the grass, more like
every grass blade is not quite good enough

You said as much, in so so many words
That was your Earthbound permanent grievance

I could not help having hope, rebelling
against how your world had hurt you

Dad, you just have to choose better blades
Dad, they're leaves, not blades
Dad, can't we just blast off?

And yet, you would surprise me
with your ebullience, how you made
everyone laugh at your best friend's funeral,
a gift to the room

Other times, enthusiasm, optimism, and wisdom
could quickly turn to a blazing criticism
of the way things worked

My orbits around you could not complete,
            reversed,
                        wobbled,
                                    sought relativity

Before the aphasia, we visited the Space Museum,
the Gemini capsule tiny and bare

You looked proud, you, the little guy
from a Philly trailer park who helped build *that!*

You've been so good at so many things,
and I'll keep trying to thank you
while you can take the words in

I see you now, mom gone too quickly,
your new wife trying to soothe you seven years on

Memory fading, and your words – all those words –
flown, though still in my cortices

Now that the snakes really are here,
and you were somewhat right,
I sit at your breakfast table

Looking over, you and she struggle
with the TV remote, stand looking out at the pool

Its green funk fading,
you finally hired the right guy

And in your confusion at these efforts,
I see your young dog and your old cat
moving closer to you both

Not begging, doing a slow prance
of proximity to you,
seeking closeness

It's a still life in motion,
a quadrangle of souls joined
by gravity's obliviousness to our goals
and wounds and accomplishments and history

Particles and spaceships and love magnetized

All these years I missed it,
that beyond the words machine-gunning
out of you in your mission to share your pain,
to bind it to us in some way that lessens,
lessons, connects you to us,
I see in the drift that pulls the pets to you
that there is only one true thing,
so simple as to make me feel stupid,
as simple as the trust the blades of grass deserved,
as simple as the lightness of those sweet paws
at your feet –

togetherness

Those astronauts would have wanted
more seats in the capsule,
more leaves cozied together,
more is better

Longevity

These are the days of my past death
Slung over a shoulder that broke
Before, brittled by gravity
And the needling pokes of the horde
And their sluicing for benefit

I want more from less in these days
To hide my bones from your fat map
Of needless points –

to walk,

lighter

Rubedo

I have woven
a parachute out of everything broken
—William Stafford

Ministration

My last words will be, “I’m sorry.”
I won’t say that aloud.
I’ll say something kind.
Inside I’ll see the vase I did not fill.
Or maybe I emptied it. Or did not tend to it.
The endless pulse pull of how I was not,
  did not, knew not.

The first kiss told me I would always fail.
The first cry of air, too.
The pulse of all that is needed and wanted
  will beat beyond my own.
I’ll know I had not kept up,
  even as I tend to you at my last.

Ascension

(After "Drinking There" *by Mark Nepo)*

In ascension
To a place confabulated
Like green on green
Becomes our dream of
A treasured crystal contrast
Perhaps aqua is what we seek
Laid over the green below

Not death, unless
We want it to be
But perhaps flight above this
Past this
An expansion beyond our tongues
And skin

But slow
Because that left behind is
Still us

We allow the kernel –
  that essential bead of self –
  which was hidden –
To debut
In slow motion
To splay the crusts of each disguise
Creaking with pain, yes,
  and over and over, blinking
Innocently into the new

Practice

I hear a father carrying a child
You're getting heavy.
The boy says *No you're not, you're fine.*

Such exquisite perfection
in the child's corralling
of the essential love tie
needed to sustain his all,

Replacing I with You
    and
Voicing You and I as the same
    and
We and You and I
    are fine because
it doesn't matter Who is Who
    and that
the dusk is beautiful and the asphalt is ugly
and the heat is radiating a bit too much
as he tousles the boy's hair and they romp
along toward some store and the boy is
secure, tending to and practicing
some form of the bond that is critical
for his every hot breath with everyone
everywhere forever.

My Happy Cavewoman

I look better than I am.
She knows why,
  my happy cavewoman,
    my shadow.

See my smile?
You must look closely.
Trudging along, it is veiled by the Sun's
  tinged orange yellow of some pine fire.

She sees.

These worries of mine came before.
And I am a carrier,
here by some of her grace, of her hope,
  filtered pure out of that Sun's kiss
  now, and way back then.

You see, back when enough push
  pushed you and me to here,
  given a chance
  to filter out more.

To make the golden rays clearer.

I look better than I am, yes,
  but don't forget my cavewoman
  way back then…

She knows.

When the Sun hits her face,
  she sees a shimmer of growth ahead,
  but less pent
  than what tips us over now.

She sees a way to tip us back up.
Through me,
  through this child I carry,
    in me.

Moderate Creatures

The fangs and sinew of our darkest minds
Pixelled, printed
Flaunted at us like needed nutrients
News of the whirled
Poison from a tie and a hairdo

And yet,
The numbers tell us
The 4-minute mile
  is only 15 miles per hour
The 100-pound human grip strength
  is limited by our bone brittleness
The human canine sharpness
  is only 20% of the lion's

But…
The fangs and sinew, right?

And yet,

.

.

.

.

.

A slip is caught by a hand before a fall
A fall is lifted by hands before a shiver
A shiver is calmed by arms before a freeze
A freeze is warmed by a body before a collapse
A collapse is enveloped by an attunement before a shutdown
  And a shutdown is averted
    by the accumulated attention,
      the natural turning toward,
        the reach, the mellifluous tonal sigh,
          the open eyes and mind, listening,
            containing, soothing, rescuing,
              repairing, protecting, feeding…
                a pull as automatic as a breath,
                  to join in bonded continuation
                    of what mortal wisps remain

Centered

(For my daughters)

The young child asks why the heart
  is to the left and not centered.
The parent smiles.
Where would you like it to be?
I want it perfect. In the middle.
Nothing is perfect, honey.
After a pause, the child cries.
But we are!
The parent fears for the child's future.
Hugs the child.
Yes, yes we are.

Years later the parent laments
  having missed the blinked moment
  when the child's slippery clear vision
  of all that is was shining and warm
  and smiling and embracing
  and was in reach, not just hoped for,
  but owned.

Somewhere, at the same time, the grown child
  is seen sitting at a red light, staring
  too long at nothing, blank, weakened,
  until a horn honks them
  into compliance.

Years later, at the end, the parent sees a scene:

The young child asks why the heart
  is to the left and not centered.
The parent smiles.
Where would you like it to be?
I want it perfect. In the middle.
Where is yours?
To the left.
Mine too, how's yours working?
Good, I guess.
Let's see…

The parent puts a hand over the child's heart,
  the child does the same to the parent.

And in this final vision of the parent,
  past when the thousand previous laments
  had hardened to regrets,
  then melted to absolution's release,
  no word is spoken.

At Dawn

Dearheart
The twining green over
What is left of you
Clambers for your essence
Your essential…
You're essential

For what you birth
Through the loamy mead
Contains, but pales to
Your essence…
You are essence

The Draft Above

The bird's long winged stride
Languid in its confidence
Betrays a privileged foresight
Its grace unencumbered by the inevitable

I watch it and know it knows
And I covet its calm
My eyes like an infant's
Pulling to metabolize that

Against this

Between

(For Ezra Pound)

The petal waits for the wind

Then rises, paling as the scorching bright above
washes its color to white…

Only to float down into shade
where its pigment returns

Joining the earth with a hue of renewal
not singed by the heat

An Affirmation of the Alchemy of Blood

In the fields and streets and houses
and schoolrooms of Pennsylvania,
I felt their sadness and depression was
trying to recruit me. But I had not entered
this living world feeling that way.

At age five, my friend's father asked me,
"What is the meaning of life?"
I said, not flippantly, "Life."
He said, "Wrong, it's love."

I carried anger toward him for a long time
for his bluntness. And even at that age I knew
he was not being gentle enough.

I think we were both right. But because I
was blessed with a healthy body and an
active and imaginative mind and soul, all
of which could buoyantly soak up the
electrifying gleam of all soft and hard and
gently folded things... Life to me was
easier than Love would become as I grew.

Love being hard doesn't mean his answer
was wrong. His answer is universally
accepted. But the pressure of recruitment
into others' sadness and depression was
an affront to the magic of being alive and
being this thing, this breathy font of light.

Or was it an affront? Can't we just witness,
shakily enough to bond,
but not become?

That is Love.

We are naturally, relationally, pulled into
others' sadness, depression, anger,
suffering… And, yes, Joy.

So I must not forget that, like a virus,
exploration and creativity and learning
and openness can recruit others as much
as sadness and depression. Even
concurrently.

I must make a choice at every recruitment
station, every minute of the day, with
every single person.

I must grow up.

After Admitting the Faults of my Rage

The young
Are smarter than I was
When I was smart

Thank God
They will need it for sure
If still there's will

Go forth
Your beauty rings a bell
Sound your beauty

Resist
The fortune of deceit
Love is fortune

Do die
In clever sighs of peace
Remain clever

Or fight
With vision much too bright
For their vision

Blind them
Tie clarity to force
Push clarity

Open
Their eyes to their own sight
Theirs are your eyes

Share eyes
Both seeing the heart's needs
Equal seeing

Of gems
The grace of potential
Collective grace

Ferenczi's Cat

(For Sándor Ferenczi and Elizabeth Severn)

My purr is not an intrusion
It's a call to you
A reward for your proximity
As you stay and stay
And stay
Until by your own means or
  to fight their judgment
You gently step back

Only to return
With your unevading eye
  and your stroke that elicits
With agreement
My returned gesture

Your bond is not a collusion
With me or to her
Unless we label our commitment
To the work and work
And work
As the gleaming jewel of
  your hypothesis –
Your motherly heart

Only to withstand
With your invariant view
  of the spirit's pliant strengths
Their bald rebukes
To continue on

Her mode is not obfuscation
It is a fundament
To the you and her and me and all
To the love the love
The love
And the doublet's power
  to heal in concert
With harmony's grace

Only to pass on
By your warm blood's rebellion
  against its own hot wisdom
And to leave me
Knowing you fully

Quantum Entanglement

Your membrane expands
Its shimmer seduces them
They don't want contraction

Your tautness hides pain
Its hardness envelops them
They long for protection

Your warning's not heard
Its subtlety eludes them
They long for connection

So do you

So...

They don't want to lose you
Your first crack splinters
Its vibrations alert them

They pivot by instinct
Your facade scatters
Its stark chaos invites them

They see and come to you
Your structure crumbles
Its false beauty allows them

To love you

Faded Color Scan, In Memoriam

My mother's gentle knock-kneed stance
Heartbreaks me every time
Young, with a hat
Her humble smile at Aunt Helen's pool
The only honeymoon they could afford

So new, you, a step above poor
  and carrying, growing a life

Why do I paw at that muted simplicity
  when it's possible now, here?
Not possible.

You showed me acorns and a squirrel at a cold park
Your beige belted coat a plan against the rain
You were learning. You were good.

Twenty-one and another coming
Maybe our last outing alone?
You worked so hard and did so well

Why do I long so deeply if you fed
  so lovingly into my trench of murky needs?

Much later I saw you staring off
Calm and more serious than you showed us
  at backyard barbecues
Please come back and tell me

Days of Telomeres

(After Erik Erikson's Eight Psychosocial Life Stages)

What gull is this?
Skating the wind shear above me
Staring down
Head tilted in wisdom's stillness
Assuming I'm ponderous over the sea's beauty
But I'm grasping at the waves
Birth behind, death ahead

Eight stages to tranche
How does it know I seek its wisdom
  in the Eights?
The foam at my bony feet
Below what's left of my knees' integrity
Or my soul's?
As I try not to let the wave's flat receding tail
Be my despair

No one comes out alive, they say
I might!

*

*

*

*

*

*

*

In the Sevens
I could generate as before
When germing, seeding, building
Hands dervishing to restore or bloom infinite things
Was the thing
Leaning into the blue wind of the long middle
Days ahead and behind
Not still, nor stagnated
Voicing the moist glossal gymnastics that land well
And stick to younger others with the confidence
And poise and care
Of the stoic

I spent years as that generative fuse
But the chinked-together telo-lengths will drop off
With the days
Still, I show the gull that

*

*

*

*

*

*

*

In the Sixes
I was
Once intimate
De-isolated
I accepted the toil
Of the close breath
The sweat in the webbing of our entwined fingers
Pulling each other to our nested goal
Faint gurgles and padding feet thumps
And a million unchoked feelings in their young faces
   and bigger bodies
The way this translational wire
Turned that proximal love toward the world – oh, how this works!
Love close, love general!

*

*

*

*

*

*

In the Fives
I do half-baked pre-frontal swordfighting with fully-baked testes
An essay on authenticity written
  in a Camaro
Trying to be big with small blood lumber
I'm a topiary
Trimmed by shears I want to mangle
Wrong bush
"Identify the identity of your bush, sir."
I'm a tree, fuck off, love me
My branches reach for a self
The fidelity of some acceptance
But girls cars muscles music enemies books heroes dreams
Faceted choices
Why are the quarterback's legs so perfectly bowed?
Their shadow dwarfing my knocked knees
Mocking the role confusion of their one job: simply bend
Lower your shoulders
"Why so tense?"
Achin' to be

I'm not sure I survived that one

*

*

*

*

*

In the Fours
C– to A+ if the lady gets stern and the multiplication tables stick
  to my glials
Elementary innocence
A flute and a revolutionary war song in a stiff suit
Spacey-minded smarts get smacked
Thrown into lockers, bathroom stall kicked open
No shitting at school anymore but
If you ever wondered,
  yes it makes one inferior to shit your pants in class
Because you're afraid to shit in the stall
But, oh, yay, 'cause my industrious grades held anyway
Once I wiped clean
Middle school monstrosities
And Dad got me a Honda motorbike
Gasoline and a helmet and a drumset bloomed competence
Still, I will go back and fucking kill them all

*

*

*

*

*

*

In the Threes
The slope of the toddler walk straightens now
My spine initiates proxy initiative
To perform the sugar magic of being
4 to 6 years old is rainbow oil on water
   and cricket chirps and air and home and
   blurry sprints till falls don't hurt
   and I know I can fly! because because because!
And school is scary even with the sniff stink
   of new erasers in vinyl pencil bags
Poor test score guilt and soft pranked meanness
Feel hot in the cheek – yes just one – 'cause
I'm cheeked against a cold pole crying in winter
   when mom is late to pick me up but
I've got my poster project rolled up in a wet fist
Purpose snips at my innocence
   as this kinder is gardened

*

*

*

*

*

*

In the Twos
I must've toddled
Wooden floor autonomy
Jackie gave me a cream mint in my high chair
Taste smell stare from the Philly porch
Into the overcast
All adults big to me but now I know
So young, they did me OK
They say you can't remember age 2
They say I'm amazing when I can
Later it's shameful to be amazing
Shamed by the tribal doubts
But I will will will! be a person
And not a maze of self-rejecting esteem?
Good luck with that
Give him a gift of some gentle bird
  whose eyes tell him this heaven will go on

*

*

*

*

*

*

In the Ones (here the weeping begins)
The weeping, now
The howling, then
The wrinkled collapsed buttocks and pointy head emerge
Smelling like God's own sweet soil
My wail of hoped trust arcing in blue
Forward, to now
To my salt-water splintering boniness in the Eights
Predicting my current mistrust, sleuthing for that hope
Peering in both directions, you and me,
  detectives meeting every day
On our longevity slide rule – stages 8-1-1-8 –
more you, more me –
Circadian
Until the feared crime of abandonment might be overtaken
By the tufty roots of secure hope – trust, grace,
  and release…

*

*

*

*

*

*

The gull banks away to leave me in silence
Confident in the integrity of its assessment
To which I am blind
  and deaf to the waves' coded froth
I'm suspended now
As if despair might smite me into the next
Or wisdom might glide me, timeless, along
  and along.

The Yielding

(For A. and T.)

This is not the fray to join
To not,
    is my hidden whispered chant
    a talismanic choir
    angels of detachment
My tool

But then you, born into now
Tiny
To you, this cradle
    springs softly
Over the edge looms
    hope only
Jeweled sprigs of everything to be
A different choir
From mine
In you

Our eyes see facets of the same crystal
Differently
Oh, my, how I prefer your fresh genius!
I defer
For you, I will reattach

I will be warm
    and still
        against your shiver
In the fray

M

Last words, the ping of the soul through
suboptimal flesh. M did it well. A single word.
Like a dollop of sweet. Like a soft pat
on the shoulder. An embrace receding.

His breaths slowing, our questions not spoken,
not in a timeline…

…will you be ok will we be ok are you ready
is it better this way do you know we will miss you
will you miss us has it been good will you be with us
do you know we will be with you
do you know your goodness
do you know we love you
do you know we know you love us

do you know we regret this… fear this… accept this…
do you?…

…simultaneous, despairing, then gently cinched
in the warm silk whisper of M's final word…

"Yes"

Acknowledgments

In the tunnel of trance over the last years of writing, I was lucky enough to benefit from the guiding eyes and bright feedback of many people as these poems formed. My warm thanks go to g. Lyn Cisneros, Jean-Marie Martz, Kamran Eshtehardi, Vincent Liota, William Preston, Bob Mirales, Brenda Blatt, Marc Duncan, Saimir Thano, Bryan Rasmussen, Ned Truslow, Patricia Kaminski, Kurt Heydle, Pierre Smith, Colleen Warnesky, Richard Schenkman, Carver Koella, Jay Brecker, Federico Muchnik, Marcel Camargo, Rick Parks, Brian Beck, Richard Shindell, Randy Noblitt, and John Walsh. And to Carol, Caitlin, and Melinda: thank you for chiming in and for tolerating my spaciness. To Avalon and Tristan for demonstrating the power of continuance. I also send gratitude to those who have passed too early: Larry Brooks, PhD, for his early support; Jeffrey Tirengel, PsyD, MPH and Ron E. Fránco Duran, PhD for upping me to this self later in life; Mark Neely, for a long-ago moment; and Nick Tanis, who taught me many life-saving things about the art of the human lens.

Thanks also go to Frederick T. Courtright at The Permissions Company on behalf of the William Stafford Estate and Archives and Graywolf Press for their gracious permission to use Mr. Stafford's words in the fourth section heading here.

And thank you to Roger and the team at Union Printing Company, LTD, for their patient guidance.

"Flaw" appeared in a different format in 2014 as a recipient of the Jim Stophel Scholarship at the California School of Professional Psychology at Alliant International University.

This book is set in Adobe Garamond, Adelle Sans Devanagari, and Source Sans Variable fonts.

Wealtown Press is committed to the principle that creative output evolves from mind, body, spirit, psychological, and collective and individual consciousness pathways. Protecting the freedom of this universal modality is crucial.

This book is printed in China by Union Printing Company, LTD, on acid-free paper.

Wealtown Press is located in the Pasadena area of California, the traditional and current homeland of the Gabrielino-Tongva peoples.

wealtownpress.com